On home ground: a Morris Cowley Occasional Four on Magdalen Bridge, Oxford, in 1924. Longwall Street, where the first Bullnose was assembled in 1912, is just beyond the buildings of Magdalen College on the right.

The Bullnose Morris

Jonathan Wood

A Shire book

CONTENTS

THE BULLNOSE MORRIS

Bull-nose, the original rendering, was informally and retrospectively applied during the 1930s to the Morris cars built between 1913 and August 1926. It is believed to be a corruption of 'Bullet-nose Morris', because the brass radiator of the original Oxford resembles a .303 rifle cartridge rather than a bull's muzzle.

ACKNOWLEDGEMENTS

This Shire Album would not have been possible without enthusiastic support and assistance from Robin Barraclough and Peter Seymour, historians of the Bullnose Morris, to whom I give my grateful thanks, though I alone am responsible for any conclusions reached. I also much appreciate the help of David Hutchison, of the Early MG Society. The Bullnose Morris Club's *Early Morris Cars* was an invaluable reference source. Illustrations were kindly supplied by Robin Barraclough, the Bullnose Morris Club, the Early MG Society, Brian Folkard, Gerry Killey, Peter Seymour and Donald Way.

Cover: *A Morris advertisement featuring the Oxford saloon for 1926, with Barker headlamp dipping system and Calometer water temperature indicator, on the front cover of 'The Motor's' first Motor Show issue dated 29th September 1925. (Robin Barraclough)*

British Library Cataloguing in Publication Data: Wood, Jonathan. The bullnose Morris. – (A Shire album; no. 359) 1. Morris automobile – History. I. Title 629.2'222. ISBN 0 7478 0491 5.

Editorial Consultant: Michael E. Ware, former Director of the National Motor Museum, Beaulieu.

Printed in Great Britain by CIT Printing Services Ltd, Press Buildings, Merlins Bridge, Haverfordwest, Pembrokeshire SA61 1XF.

William Morris, Viscount Nuffield, a still sprightly eighty-year-old, talks to Bullnose Morris owners at Cowley in August 1958. The occasion was a 'Daily Express' competition to find the oldest privately owned Morris. The winner, motoring artist Frank Wootton, received a new Morris Minor. A great philanthropist, Morris donated some £30 million to charity and was made a baronet in 1929, a baron in 1934 and a viscount in 1938.

THE CAR FROM COWLEY

William Morris's famous Bullnose became Britain's most popular car when in 1923 it toppled the Model T Ford from the position it had occupied for eleven years. Yet, paradoxically, the car from Cowley created by the intensely patriotic Morris was a Yankee at heart.

With no financial resources, Morris had begun his career by assembling bicycles at the family home and as a consequence he was fortunate not to inherit the proud but misguided British engineering tradition that required a manufacturer to design and make as much of a product as possible within his own factory. This belief was exemplified by Herbert Austin, Morris's great rival of the inter-war years.

Bereft of this distraction and so flying in the face of industrial orthodoxy, Morris pragmatically assembled his vehicles from bespoke parts produced by others, a more demanding discipline, in much the same way that car factories operate today. This policy, coupled with an instinctive feel for automobile design and, crucially, a formidable financial flair, helped to make him the most successful, and richest, British motor manufacturer of his day.

Although William Richard Morris (1877–1963) is always associated with Oxford and its suburb of Cowley, he was born in Worcester. But both his parents came from the Oxford area and in 1880 the family returned to the district, settling in the parish of Cowley St John, then a village on the south-eastern outskirts of the university city.

Morris was to display a strong affinity for mechanical matters and, after education

William Morris's home at 16 James Street, Cowley, in 2000. A plaque, to the right of the front door, indicates its famous former occupant. Morris displayed his bicycles in the right-hand window or, on sunny days, in the front garden. The Cowley-built Maestro hatchback in the foreground bears the name of his Austin rival, the two makes becoming allied through the creation, in 1952, of the British Motor Corporation.

at the local church school, which he left in 1893 at the age of fifteen and a half, he spent nine months working for an Oxford bicycle agent, leaving when his employer refused to increase his weekly wage from five to six shillings.

Returning home to 16 James Street, and with a borrowed capital of £4, he began to repair and sell bicycles. In 1894 he started to assemble his own from proprietary components in a gas-lit slate-roofed brick lean-to in his father's back garden. Such was Morris's success as a 'cycle maker' that from 1900 he was able to rent a shop at 48 High Street – Oxford's main thoroughfare. He soon expanded into some old livery stables, shared with a greengrocer, at nearby 100 Holywell Street, which he used for bicycle repairs.

From 1901 William Morris progressed to producing motorcycles and later, in 1903, came the grandly named 'Oxford Automobile and Cycle Agency'. This had been established by a local businessman, Frank Barton, with Launcelot Creyke, a wealthy former Oxford undergraduate, and Morris became works manager. Unfortunately the business foundered in April 1904 because of Creyke's extravagance and Morris suffered the indignity of having to buy his tools back at the liquidator's sale, held in the pouring rain. He never forgot the experience and vowed thereafter to retain complete control of his business.

Soon back at Holywell Street, he ran a motor hire service from what was named 'The Oxford Garage' and began to sell new cars from there. His agencies included the British marques Belsize, Humber, Singer and Standard, together with the newly introduced Hupmobile from the United States.

The business prospered: by 1910 a site had been purchased nearby at 20 Longwall Street and the new premises with a fine brick neo-classical frontage, which still survives, were named 'The Morris Garage'. It was an impressive endorsement of its owner's resilience and business acumen. Soon afterwards, in 1913, it became 'The Morris Garages (W. R. Morris, Proprietor)'.

By 1910, as he later recalled, 'I became convinced that there was going to be a big demand for a popularly priced car. What had happened about bicycles I felt sure would happen with cars.' But he 'deplored the hold USA motor products were obtaining in Great Britain'. He had in mind the value-for-money Model T Ford that was beginning to dominate the market and from 1911 would be mass-produced at Trafford Park, Manchester.

Having been in the motor trade since 1903, William Morris was in a perfect position to evaluate the merits and shortcomings of the cars that passed through his hands. Between 1910 and 1912 he was absorbed in the creation of a small car that was to be named the Morris Oxford. Its keynote features would be reliability and low running

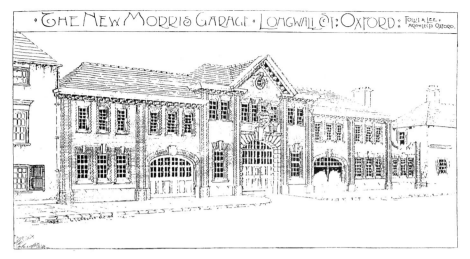

'One of the best appointed Garages in the kingdom' declared this advertisement for The Morris Garage in the 1910 'Oxford Yearbook'. Opened in Longwall Street that year, the first Bullnose was built there in 1912 and Morris contemplated limited production on this site but moved instead to Cowley.

costs. Morris was thus in the vanguard of the popular light car movement. In 1912 a 'light car' was defined as a vehicle with an engine capacity limited to 1500 cc.

But its production would be constrained by his lack of financial resources and he had little choice but to follow the practice he had adopted from his days as a bicycle maker. A shrewd and perceptive buyer, Morris planned to assemble rather than manufacture the car and to order its purpose-designed component parts from specialist engineering companies.

Morris also held an agency for the White & Poppe carburettor produced by a Coventry-based proprietary engine manufacturer founded in 1899 by Alfred White, a local businessman who had successfully made the transition from making watches to bicycles, and a Norwegian engineer, Peter Poppe. At the suggestion of another White & Poppe agent, William Burgess, the Oxford garage proprietor approached the company and it undertook the design, to Morris's brief, of the car's mechanicals. Time

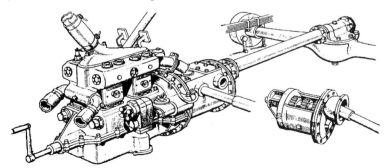

The Standard Oxford's White & Poppe engine, three-speed gearbox and torque tube transmission to the Wrigley overhead worm-driven rear axle. The inset shows the gearbox and propeller shaft. A later alternative to the Bosch magneto illustrated was the Mea, also German-made.

was short, and in the summer of 1912 Poppe left Coventry with key members of his team for his native Norway, where they could work without interruption and away from prying eyes.

In the small town of Horten, some 35 miles (56 km) south of Oslo, a drawing office was established above a shop occupied by Poppe's nephew, L. O. Firing, who was a naval tailor. The premises were owned by Firing's mother, Peter Poppe's sister, and it was in these unlikely surroundings that the engine, gearbox and chassis of the car took shape.

With work proceeding apace, Morris registered his car company on 2nd August 1912 under the name of W. R. M. Motors Ltd, reflecting his initials. As ever, finance was a problem and, despite his reservations, Morris accepted backing from twenty-four-year-old George Loveden William Henry Parker, the seventh Earl of Macclesfield, whom he had met during the latter's undergraduate years at Christ Church college. The Earl lived near Watlington, not far from Oxford. As the largest investor, he owned £4000 worth of preference shares. Morris could now place an initial order with White & Poppe for three hundred engines at £45 apiece and confirmed it by paying a 10 per cent deposit of £1350.

The chassis was produced by Rubery Owen whilst the front and rear axles and steering gear were the work of Birmingham-based E. G. Wrigley. Bodywork came from nearer to home, being supplied by the established Oxford coachbuilder Charles Raworth & Sons.

Delays in the production of the engine prevented Morris from exhibiting his car at the 1912 London Motor Show. Instead he displayed a set of blueprints on his empty stand, where they impressed Gordon Stewart of the London motor agents Stewart & Ardern, who had established his business only the previous year. Although a subsidiary to Burgess, now Morris's South of England agent, he ordered no fewer than four hundred Oxfords.

The prototype Morris Oxford was built at Longwall Street in 1912 and a limited number of cars could have been assembled there. But, encouraged by Stewart's order, Morris decided to rent the former Oxford Military College in Hollow Way, Temple Cowley, a three-storey building that had been empty since 1905. Only about $1^1/2$ miles

Whilst all the single-storey buildings that Morris erected in the 1920s have been demolished, perversely, the former Oxford Military College of 1876, which he used for car production between 1913 and 1919, has survived. Vacated by the College in 1896, it was occupied from 1899 until 1905 by Alfred Breese Ltd, which made braces and New Road bicycles there. Breese may have had plans for car production as the former drill ground had been adapted as a 'trial track for motor cars'.

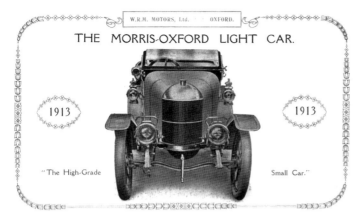

THE MORRIS-OXFORD LIGHT CAR.

W.R.M. MOTORS, Ltd.   OXFORD.

1913   1913

"The High-Grade   Small Car."

The Oxford, as it appeared in Morris's 1913 catalogue. The 'unique V shaped radiator' was produced by the Coventry-based Doherty Motor Components and the headlamps were from Powell & Hanmer. The Wrigley-made front axle was designed by that company's Frank Woollard, who from 1923 to 1931 ran Morris Engines.

(2.4 km) from his former home, the building, which he secured at the end of 1912, became the Cowley Motor Works, and he was later able to buy the property.

In truth it was a far from satisfactory structure. Machining was undertaken on the ground floor, static chassis were assembled on the first, and they were united with their bodies on the top storey. These components parts and completed cars were laboriously transported, from one floor to the other, on rope-operated lifts.

In 1914 the first of an extensive range of more suitable single-storey structures, the 'new steel building', was built behind the works on what had been the college's former parade ground. However, most of the development at Cowley took place after the First World War and was to the south; by 1926 Morris's factories covered over 40 acres (16 hectares) of land.

The first car had been exhibited at the North of England Motor Show held in Manchester in February 1913, although the engine's cylinder block was a wooden dummy. In the following month, on 28th March, Gordon Stewart collected the first

This 1913 Oxford illustrates the limitations of the two-seater bodywork as the elderly gentleman is almost completely occupying the sole bench-type seat! Sankey was responsible for the steel artillery wheels, Morris sharing the £720 cost of the die with Cecil Bayliss, designer of the Birmingham-built Perry.

production Oxford from Cowley. William Morris was on his way.

Unlike many of his contemporaries, he made no attempt to disguise the fact that the Morris Oxford was powered by a 'bought-in' engine. Such cars, invariably powered by a unit of its *supplier's* conception, tended to be branded as 'cheap and nasty', but the Oxford was neither and White & Poppe's contribution was duly credited in *The Autocar's* description published in April 1913. Progressively, the engine and gearbox were mounted in unit, like the Model T, which speeded and cheapened the production process.

Peter Poppe's four-cylinder 1018 cc unit, with a 60 by 90 mm bore and stroke, was a sound, if rather dated, design in being a T-head engine that was also relatively expensive to manufacture. It accordingly used two camshafts rather than the single one of the increasingly popular L-head or side-valve layout.

In common with most British cars of the day, although not the ubiquitous Ford, which had a removable cylinder head, it featured a monobloc non-detachable one. The cast-iron block also neatly incorporated the inlet and exhaust manifolds and was mounted on an aluminium crankcase.

The timing gears were at the back of the unit and on the nearside invariably drove a Bosch ZF4 magneto that ignited sparking plugs from the same German manufacturer. Perversely, the engine would run on little else!

The three-bearing crankshaft was splash-lubricated and the drive passed through no fewer than thirty-six alternate steel and bronze clutch plates, which ran in the engine's oil. The gearbox, a three-speed unit with the obligatory right-hand change, was supported by a tube that passed through its casing and braced the chassis. Suspension was by half-elliptic springs at the front with long rear three-quarter elliptics.

Morris was influenced by the Hupmobile in his adoption of enclosed torque tube transmission, although this was probably in turn inspired by the Model T, Robert Hupp having previously worked for Ford. An overhead worm-driven rear axle was used.

The handsome gilled tube brass radiator was distinctive and what we now call the 'bullnose' type. As Morris always took a particular interest in radiator design, he can

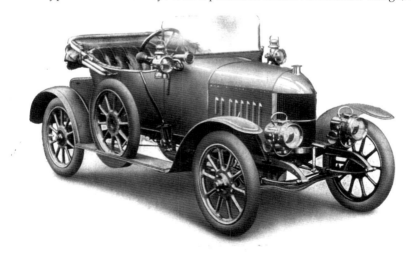

The De Luxe Oxford for 1914 with a wider track, longer wheelbase and larger radiator than the original, and, at £195, it cost £20 more. The body was accordingly more comfortable and better finished. Domed rather than flat mudguards were fitted.

Peter Poppe of White & Poppe, designer of the Oxford's engine, with his wife's top-of-range De Luxe drophead coupé by Raworth. Note the electric, rather than acetylene, headlamps, although they are fitted with wartime masks. It was upholstered in Bedford cord. There was an alternative non-catalogued version by Hollick & Pratt.

probably be credited with its agreeably curved contours. That there was only one body style, an open two-seater finished in pearl grey, reflected the short wheelbase of just 7 feet (2133 mm). The price was £175.

Rated at 8.9 hp, the new Morris proved to be a lively, reliable performer with a high-revving, economical and torquey engine and it would happily cruise at 40 mph (64 km/h). A few shortcomings were soon rectified. Uncertain steering was put down to the track and after about 150 cars had been completed this was increased from 40 to 42 inches (1016 to 1066 mm) and the layout of the steering linkages was revised. Minor modifications were also made to the clutch.

Yet further improvements were incorporated when Morris unveiled the supplementary Oxford De Luxe at the 1913 London Motor Show for the 1914 season. At this point the original car became the Standard model.

With the De Luxe, Morris further addressed the steering problem that was still afflicting the Standard by increasing the track, once again, to 45 inches (1143 mm). He simultaneously introduced an Elliot-type front axle in place of the Standard's more orthodox reversed Elliot. A longer-wheelbase chassis (7 feet 6 inches, or 2286 mm), roomier, more curvaceous coachwork and a larger radiator also featured. The popular two-seater tourer was priced at £195.

Ambitiously, there were now four bodies on offer: a two-seater, a sports version with aluminium single-seater body, a coupé and a van body with mahogany panelling.

In 1914 Morris built 907 cars, which established him as a medium-sized car maker, numerically more successful than Austin (355) and Vauxhall (529) but still a long way behind Ford, which was Europe's biggest producer, with 8352 Model Ts completed.

The last Standard, renamed the Popular for 1915 on being enhanced with the De Luxe body, was built during the First World War in October 1915 and the final De Luxe did not leave Cowley until March 1917. In all 1475 White & Poppe engined Oxfords were completed, 495 Standards and 980 De Luxes, and they decisively outsold their Singer and Hillman rivals.

By this time WRM Motors had introduced a new model, which was named the Cowley. It would enable William Morris to realise his ambition of overhauling the Model T as Britain's most popular car.

AMERICAN POWER

In 1913, the year in which the Oxford entered production, Morris realised that he had made a fundamental mistake in its planning. Because of the short wheelbase it was only possible to accommodate two-seater coachwork, but the family man required four seats. Morris may have conceived the Oxford to meet his own particular needs; he had married in 1904 but he and his wife never had any children.

Four seats meant a larger car with a more powerful engine. Morris therefore asked White & Poppe to produce a 1.5 litre 60 by 100 mm version of its existing T-head design. Unfortunately the price of about £50 for the engine and attendant gearbox would have made the resulting model unacceptably expensive. If he was to attain his ambition of challenging the Ford, selling for just £135, the new model would have to be more competitively priced.

But then, in its issue of 7th January 1914, *The Motor Trader* carried details of a small four-cylinder engine being developed in the United States by the Continental Motor Manufacturing Company of Detroit. Whether or not William Morris read this report is not known but early in 1914 he sailed for the USA and, once there, presented himself at Continental's newly opened Jefferson Avenue works. There he was quoted a price of just £25 for the projected engine and, on his return to Britain and armed with Continental's drawings, he attempted to get White & Poppe to produce a similar unit, but the Coventry firm could not match the Americans' price.

However, White & Poppe's chief draughtsman, Hans Landstad, proposed that he and Morris should return to Detroit, where he would secure a job with Continental, which was well on its way to becoming the largest independent supplier of proprietary engines in the USA. In 1915 it would deliver some 46,000 units, which contrasted with the one thousand or so being built every year by White & Poppe. High volumes clearly spelt lower unit costs.

Morris agreed and in April 1914 they sailed for the USA on the *Mauretania*. During the voyage the self-taught Oxford motor manufacturer and the Norwegian engineer,

The Continental Motor Manufacturing Company's Detroit factory in Jefferson Avenue, where the Model U engine used by Morris was produced. The plant, designed by Albert Kahn, who was responsible for Ford's Highland Park works, covered 12 acres (4.8 hectares) and opened in 1912. This factory and the firm's Muskegon works were jointly capable of producing fifty thousand engines a year.

Left: *The nearside of Continental's remarkably modern Model U engine, as fitted in the 1915 Cowley. The monobloc block/crankcase and detachable cylinder head were well in advance of European practice, as was the centrally positioned gear lever.*

Below: *The Model U's offside with the American Zenith carburettor bolted directly to the cylinder block whilst the magneto was driven via a skew gear. The substantial aluminium sump with its fixed starting handle incorporated troughs which fed oil to the big-end bearings.*

who had begun his career in an Oslo shipyard, started work on the design of the car that was destined to make William Morris Britain's most successful motor manufacturer of his day.

Once at Continental, Morris and Landstad were able to examine its 95 cubic inches (1556 cc), 2.75 by 4 inches (69.8 by 101.6 mm) Model U Red Seal engine. Designed by its chief engineer, Cornell graduate Walter A. Frederick, it entered production early in 1915.

In the event Morris paid $85 per engine, the equivalent of £17 14s 2d, which was a third less than the original estimate. Even when shipping charges and insurance costs of £6 10s per unit were taken into account, it was still cheaper than buying them from Coventry, a mere 50 miles (80 km) or so from his Cowley factory.

He envisaged producing 2500 cars in the first year and ordered that number of engines. Three-speed gearboxes came from the Detroit Gear and Machine Company and cost him $40 or £8 6s 6d each. The axles by the Timken-Detroit Axle Company were sourced in the same city.

Whilst Landstad remained at Continental for three months, returning in October, Morris left for Britain. Soon afterwards, on 4th August, the First World War broke out and he lowered his production target to an initial 1500 cars.

The first Cowley, fitted with a pre-production engine, was completed in March 1915 and unveiled to the motoring press in April, when, once again, Morris made no secret of the origins of its component parts. Soon afterwards engines began to arrive from the United States and the first car for public sale was completed in August.

At its heart the new American unit was as modern as the White & Poppe unit used in the Oxford was by then dated. Like the Ford T, though unlike its British contemporaries, it featured a combined cast-iron block and crankcase, side valves and detachable cylinder head. An unconventional feature was the now universal dipstick.

However, the Model U's bore meant a 12.1 RAC horsepower rating that would have made potential owners liable for a £4 4s annual duty. Deviously, Morris falsified its internal dimensions, declaring them to be 69 by 100 mm, instead of 69.8 by 101.6 mm,

The four-seater Cowley, a noticeably larger car than the Oxford. This is a wartime version, as indicated by the headlamp masks. The horizontal bar on the gilled tube radiator survived on the post-war cars until 1921. Note the bench front seat, which endured until the same year.

giving 11.9 hp, so that the '1495 cc' car fell within the 6.5/12 hp band. Such vehicles were liable for £3 3s tax, a saving of £1 1s.

The three-bearing crankshaft had pressure-lubricated main bearings although the big ends relied on splash. Unlike the White & Poppe unit's complex clutch, the Continental engine used a simple dry Ferodo two-plate component.

The unit construction gearbox betrayed its American origins, as did the centrally positioned gear change which sprang from a simple ball joint rather than moving in the British manner in a visible gate and expensively operated, via rods, by the driver's right hand. It also had the virtue of being extremely easy to master and was, declared *The Autocar's* correspondent with commendable candour, 'One of the most easily operated gear changes we have ever tried'.

Like the Oxford, drive was by torque tube whilst the rear axle was 'a fine piece of work'. This was an excellent American design because the casing was made of two steel pressings welded together and is better known as the 'banjo' concept, which survives to this day. It was a considerable improvement on contemporary British axles, which were invariably heavier, made in sections and then bolted together – a time-consuming and consequently expensive process. An efficient helical-cut differential gear, the first on a British car apart from the obscure Wilson-Pilcher of 1901, also featured.

The chassis was effectively a scaled-up version of that used on the Oxford although, crucially, the 8 foot 6 inch (2590 mm) wheelbase was 1 foot (304 mm) longer than the De Luxe to accommodate the four-seater coachwork.

It was available with both two- and four-seater coachwork and at £165 the former was £34 cheaper than its Oxford De Luxe equivalent. The all-important four-seater cost £194, which was still £5 less. The bodies, which included coupé and van versions, were the work of Coventry-based Hollick & Pratt because Raworth was too small to cope with the increased production Morris had envisaged. However, in September

The 1917 engine, no. 11254, of a surviving Cowley with the unit's American origins clearly displayed on the brass plate located below the valve chest. The petrol-priming taps did not feature on the post-war Hotchkiss-built units. Morris added the Lucas E20 dynamo, which accordingly looked like an afterthought.

1915 the Chancellor of the Exchequer, Reginald McKenna, announced a 33.3 per cent duty on imported cars and parts with the result that the prices of the two- and four-seater Morris rose respectively to £194 and £222.

Production continued intermittently throughout the war with the last American-engined Cowley being delivered in November 1919. A total of 1485 was completed although, perversely, the two-seater was the most popular option, accounting for 676 examples. This compared with 476 fours, perhaps reflecting a market distorted by the absence of husbands and sons fighting on the Western Front.

Morris had, in the meantime, become absorbed with work for the war effort. He had initially obtained only modest contracts because Cowley was essentially an assembly operation and thus equipped with only a limited number of machine tools.

This situation changed dramatically in 1916 when a Royal Navy minesweeper captured intact a German mine and its sinker and the latter was found to be of a superior design to its British equivalent. The Admiralty decided to copy the concept and the manufacture of the sophisticated sinker, the part that was laid on the sea bed and kept the mine at a predetermined depth, was crucial. If the usual skilled labour was employed, output would be limited to forty a week.

Morris proposed that the sinker be instead broken down into individual components and these then be manufactured by small engineering companies. The parts could then be brought together and assembled at Cowley. In this way, he foresaw, output could be increased to 250 a week.

His plan was accepted. Arthur Rowse, a Whitworth scholar and superintending engineer for the Birmingham-based Ministry of Munitions, oversaw the breakdown of the sinker into its separate pieces. Hans Landstad designed the all-important jigs. He had joined Morris as works manager after his return from the United States, where such processes were commonplace, and he also had experience of the demanding discipline of producing interchangeable parts at White & Poppe.

Starting in September 1916, Morris was in due course manufacturing some two thousand sinkers a week. He was also able to reduce their price from £50 to £40 and, finally, £21. Eventually some 45,000 were produced. Morris's contribution to the war effort was recognised in 1917 when he was awarded the OBE.

WRM Motors was now well placed to benefit from an expected post-war boom as the Cowley was a thoroughly modern, reliable car that had the virtue of being extremely easy to drive. Its manufacture would be placed in the hands of the talented Rowse, who joined Morris as production manager. The prospects looked good.

The Morris Cowley badge.

13

A CUT ABOVE THE REST

Morris's ambitions were achieved in the 1920s when he emerged as Britain's leading and most profitable car maker. Relying on a host of suppliers, he obtained sixty days' credit from them and was able to build a Bullnose in just six; the fortunes of Morris Motors were thus built on the twin pillars of mechanical and financial engineering.

Even before peace was declared in November 1918, Morris had devised his post-war strategy. Announced in September, two models based on the Continental Cowley chassis would be offered.

The Cowley's specification was downgraded and it was transformed into a no-frills model for the mass market. Able to attain 50 mph (80 km/h) and return 28 mpg (10.2 litres/100 km), these figures also initially applied to the more expensive Oxford,

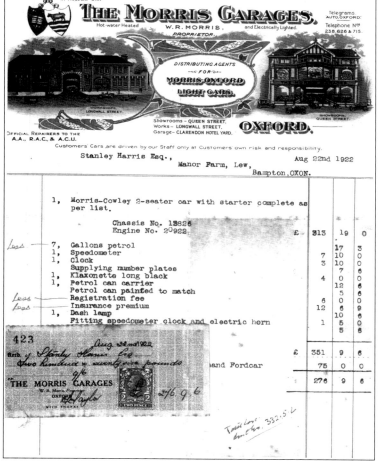

The Morris Garages' headed paper of the 1920s. The business was responsible for Bullnose distribution throughout Berkshire, Buckinghamshire and Oxfordshire. The proportions of the Longwall Street garage and Queen Street showrooms have been appropriately enhanced! In a sign of the times in 1922, Stanley Harris, on trading in his Model T Ford, was allowed £75 off the price of a new two-seater Morris Cowley.

14

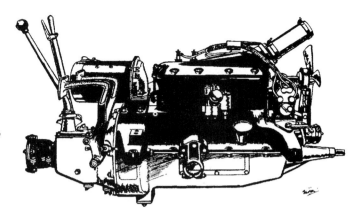

The Hotchkiss-built Morris engine of 1919, outwardly similar to the Continental Model U unit. It presented an uncluttered appearance under the bonnet because the dynamotor, a combined dynamo and starter, was introduced above the gearbox bell housing on the Oxford, so protruding into the driving compartment, a location which was retained until 1921.

which would be better finished and equipped. Its evolution is charted in the following chapter. By 1926, the last year of Bullnose production, there would be a £78 differential between the two.

Although he completed 312 Continental Cowleys in 1919, the first full year of peace, William Morris soon had to address the problem of engine supply. In Detroit, Continental had decided to discontinue the manufacture of the Model U engine because it was too small for the American market. This turned out to be a blessing in disguise as Morris no longer had to rely on a supplier located some 3500 miles (5632 km) from Cowley. Fortunately he was able to purchase the rights to the design, but he then needed an engineering company in England to copy the power unit for him.

White & Poppe was fully committed to Dennis, and other firms required a deposit that Morris was unable to pay. Then in the spring of 1919 he was visited by two executives from Hotchkiss, the French armaments manufacturer and car maker. Vincent Benet, an American, was its managing director and Henry Ainsworth was general manager of its Coventry munitions factory. When the First World War had broken out the firm had feared that its Saint-Denis works on the northern outskirts of Paris would be overrun by the Germans. It had therefore established two new arms factories, one in Lyons and the other, from May 1915, at Gosford Street, Coventry. Planned and run by Ainsworth, this works was equipped to manufacture machine-guns and, by the time the Armistice was signed, some fifty thousand of them had been completed. Demand for its Coventry-made weapons accordingly ceased almost overnight and Benet was actively looking for work to keep the plant in business. Crucially, he agreed to undertake Morris's order for engines and gearboxes at under £50 apiece without requesting a deposit.

Although the Hotchkiss-built unit outwardly resembled the American one, very few of the parts were interchangeable and there were detailed differences. One was the internal dimensions as Morris specified that the engine should become a genuine 11.9 hp. This was achieved by reducing the bore size from 69.8 to 69.5 mm. The stroke was modestly increased from 101.6 to 102 mm and the 1548 cc that resulted was a mere 8 cc less than the Continental unit.

Being a French company, Hotchkiss was tooled up to produce metric threads. These were retained but the nut and bolt hexagons were adapted to accept a British Standard spanner.

Hotchkiss's sample engines were delivered to Cowley in June and the first chassis to be so powered was completed on 18th July 1919 and destined for Australia. The

15

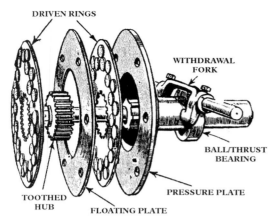

DRIVEN RINGS

WITHDRAWAL FORK

BALL/THRUST BEARING

TOOTHED HUB

FLOATING PLATE

PRESSURE PLATE

The Bullnose's distinctive cork-faced clutch, which ran in the engine's oil. This also provided essential lubrication for the dynamotor's inverted-tooth driving chain. Introduced in 1919, the concept outlived the Bullnose and Morris continued to use it, latterly in single-plate form, until 1938.

first Bullnose for the home market was dispatched to distributors W. Watson & Company of Liverpool in November.

Initially Hotchkiss copied the Continental's Ferodo-faced clutch and the first eighty-five engines were so equipped. But clutch slip, caused by engine oil leaking through the rear crankshaft seal, was experienced. Morris's response, what we would now call lateral thinking, was to let the lubricant in by drilling an oilway in the crankcase and the engine reverted to a wet clutch, as featured on the original Oxford.

Driving through two cork-faced steel plates, the result was a beautifully smooth action that further contributed to the Bullnose's driver-friendly controls. In its adoption Morris was probably influenced by the Continental-engined Hudson Super Six, which featured a similar device. Significantly, The Morris Garages had acquired an agency for the American make.

Morris was also refining the way in which he manufactured his cars. Whereas in pre-war days he had assembled the components of the Morris Oxford from large individual units, through the abilities of Arthur Rowse such items as the American axles and steering gear were also copied by British suppliers but broken down into much smaller parts. They were then assembled at Cowley in much the same way that the mine sinkers had been produced during the war. By the end of 1923 Morris had over two hundred subcontractors on his books.

He also had to address the vital matter of bodywork. Hollick & Pratt was now his

The iron foundry at Cowley was built in 1919 to ensure continuity of supply of cylinder blocks, which were then transported by lorry to Morris's Coventry engine factory. This is the Lucas continuous core drying store. However, in 1928 the foundry, which also produced gearbox casings, was moved to Coventry, a more logical location.

16

From 1920 some Bullnose bodywork was built at Cowley. In keeping with traditional coachbuilding techniques, this bodywork was timber-framed and then clad with metal. These two-seaters being panelled in the Sheet Metal Department are destined for the Cowleys of 1925.

favoured coachbuilder but it was also committed to other manufacturers and Morris believed it would be unable to cope with his requirements. A bodyshop was therefore built at Cowley on the allotments opposite the old Military College and to run it he appointed his friend Lancelot Pratt of Hollick & Pratt, who continued to manage his own business. The facility opened in 1920, initially for the production of touring bodies for the two-seater Cowley and the four-seater Oxford.

Announced in August 1919, the Cowley was available only with its factory-built two-seater body and it was not until later in 1920 that it was joined by the more popular Coventry-made four-seater. However, because of shortages of components the overwhelming majority of the 1994 cars Morris built that year were the more profitable Oxfords: 1606 of them, compared with 385 Cowleys.

Thereafter the cheaper model was in the ascendancy and in 1926, when Bullnose assembly peaked, demand for the Cowley was such that its production exceeded that of the Oxford by 2.5 to 1.

The Cowley range expanded for the 1921 season when supplementary De Luxe versions of both the two-seater and the four-seater were introduced. The two-seater Sports Cowley appeared in March.

But at the end of 1920, the industry was hit by a slump. Morris Motors, as the business had become in 1919, owed Hotchkiss a substantial £137,000, a bill it was unable to honour. Morris was saved by two stalwarts, the financier Arthur Gillett, whose Oxford bank had just been taken over by Barclays, and, again, by the Earl of Macclesfield. Later, in 1922, Morris peremptorily severed all contact with the man who had twice saved him by sending the Earl a cheque for his £25,000 investment. Displaying a ruthlessness that belied a modest demeanour, he clearly wished to be the sole master of his destiny.

With one problem solved, another soon presented itself as the economy was plunged into a severe recession in 1921 and sales stagnated. Morris's response to the crisis, announced on 9th February 1921, was to cut the price of the slow-selling Cowley four-seater tourer by £100, from an inflated £525 to £425. In later years he clearly recalled his exchanges with his general manager, Hugh Wordsworth Grey, who protested: 'But how can you do that? You are only making a profit of £15 a car'; to which Morris bit back: 'The place is full of cars and you are not making a profit at all. You are making a loss.'

His daring initiative broke the logjam. Sales rose threefold to 236 in February and increased, again, to 400 in March, to be followed by figures of 361, 352 and 361 in the following three months. The corner was turned and in October 1921 Morris again consolidated his position with further price reductions. He ended the year having produced 2994 cars, a third more than in 1920.

In 1922 the Cowley emerged as a model in its own right: hitherto it had been regarded merely as a utilitarian version of the Oxford but from then, as volumes rose, it became both cheaper and better equipped. There were new bodies, less expensive than the previous year's, with doors specified only on the nearside, the two-seater having one and the four-seater two. No sidescreens were fitted although they were subsequently offered as extras. The range was essentially the same as the previous year's, except that the coupé was discontinued.

Both the Cowley and the Oxford were also fitted with revised engines, designated the Type CB unit, for the 1922 season. This was to endure throughout the cheaper model's manufacturing life. It differed from the original CA version in having a redesigned cylinder block with four exhaust ports, which gave better gas flow. This replaced the original's three, the centre two ports having been siamesed.

Despite Morris still having Ford in his sights, the Model T's ascendancy appeared unstoppable. It dominated the market and in the fifteen months to the end of 1920 no fewer than 46,362 cars and trucks left the Manchester factory. However, this was to prove to be the high point of its British sales. From 1921 all cars on Britain's roads were liable for a horsepower tax levied at the rate of £1 per RAC horsepower, which was related to an engine's bore. The owner of a big-bored Ford, rated at 22 hp, therefore paid £22 whilst a neighbour with an 11.9 hp Morris Cowley was liable for just £12. The American car also dated back to 1908...

Morris's output was rising, with 5000 cars leaving Cowley in 1922, and the figure grew in 1923 to 14,995. It was then that William Morris achieved his ambition of overhauling the Model T Ford, and his company became Britain's largest car maker. However, the American firm built more vehicles because of its truck sales, 18,688 that year compared with 11,507 cars sold. But Morris overtook Trafford Park's total output in 1925 and he was destined to dominate the car market, the 1934–5 seasons excepted,

Testing Bullnose power units during the 1925 season at Morris Engines. Initially dynamotor driven to free them off, at 1250 rpm the engines, fuelled by town gas, took over and drove the dynamotor. Subsequently the gas was replaced by petrol.

until 1947, when he was overhauled by the Austin Company, his long-time rival.

His increasing success began to produce its own problems. In December 1922 he had bought one of his principal subcontractors, Hollick & Pratt, which built most of his bodies. Its works had burnt down on 1st August and Lancelot Pratt suggested that Morris, as his main customer, acquire the business. He did so at a cost of £100,000 and the company was renamed 'Morris Bodies'. At the same time he purchased another supplier, the Osberton Radiator Company, an Oxford-based firm established with his encouragement in 1919.

Hotchkiss was in a similar position to Hollick & Pratt but it was faced with the prospect of being unable to keep pace with the demand for Bullnose engines. Morris therefore bought it in May 1923 for £349,423, renamed it 'Morris Engines' and gave its manager, Frank Woollard, full rein. As a result production was quadrupled from 300 units a week in May 1923 to 1200 in December 1924.

Backed by a substantial £300,000 investment, Woollard created a battery of transfer

Gearboxes were similarly the subject of flow-line production methods at Coventry: this is the 'box assembly track'. They were later united with the engines and the combined units then delivered to Cowley by lorry.

The engine and gearbox store in the erecting shop at Cowley. Note the bulky dynamotor fitted to the side of the gearbox on the extreme left. It was relegated to beneath the floorboards on the Oxford in 1921 and standardised on the Cowley for 1924.

The 1922 and 1923 Cowleys were outwardly very similar although under the bonnet in the latter year a single-jet Smiths carburettor re-placed what had proved to be an unsuitable SU sloper. The doors, which lacked external handles, were fitted only on the nearside.

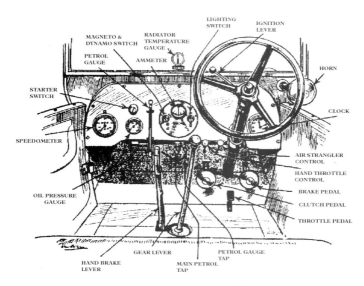

LIGHTING SWITCH

IGNITION LEVER

MAGNETO & DYNAMO SWITCH

RADIATOR TEMPERATURE GAUGE

PETROL GAUGE

AMMETER

HORN

STARTER SWITCH

CLOCK

SPEEDOMETER

AIR STRANGLER CONTROL

HAND THROTTLE CONTROL

OIL PRESSURE GAUGE

BRAKE PEDAL

CLUTCH PEDAL

THROTTLE PEDAL

GEAR LEVER

PETROL GAUGE TAP

HAND BRAKE LEVER

MAIN PETROL TAP

The dashboard of a 1924 Cowley. In those days a clock appears to have been of greater concern to the driver than the speedometer, which was more easily seen by the passenger!

20

When introduced in 1924, the Occasional Four sold for £215, which placed it between the two- and four-seater Cowleys. Its rear compartment could be used for luggage or the side-mounted folding seats could be occupied by one adult or two children.

machines that automatically produced one fully machined Bullnose cylinder block every four minutes. In all fifty-three separate machining operations were carried out and in 1924 the process was extended to the gearbox casing. Such techniques were in advance of anything else in the industrialised world, including the United States. In practice the system proved too advanced and was subsequently dismantled, only to be revived by the motor industry twenty years later.

The 1923 Cowley range was very similar to the previous year's cars although the equipment was somewhat basic, with such items as a dynamotor (see the next chapter) for starting and battery charging, speedometer, clock, oil and petrol gauges available at extra cost.

There was a new model with special coachwork named The Morris Garages Chummy, the brainchild of Cecil Kimber, its newly appointed general manager. The hood of this open two-plus-two seater, also available in Oxford guise, ingeniously protected the rear occupants from the elements. Significantly, it represented the

Another 1924 introduction was the Commercial Traveller's Cowley with the rear locker providing provision for samples. This had rather more room than the dickey compartment of a two-seater. These eight examples are leaving Cowley for delivery to the 'Daily Express'. It was produced until 1926.

The Cowley acquired a five-lamp lighting set in 1924 although the units were smaller than those used on the Oxford. This is a 1925 car with new simplified upright hood sticks.

starting point of the MG (for Morris Garages) marque.

In 1924 it was replaced by a cheaper Morris version, named the Occasional Four. Also new was the Commercial Traveller's Car with a useful luggage locker. All models benefited from a dynamotor and a complete set of instruments although there was still no wing mirror, windscreen wiper or dash lamp.

A Lucas five-lamp set replaced the original three-lamp layout although the lights were smaller than those used on the Oxford. Sidescreens were also standardised and, whilst the single-piece windscreen featured on the two-seater, this was replaced on the

The van version of the Bullnose is now dubbed the 'Snubnose' on account of its different radiator. This is a 1925 example fitted with a factory De Luxe body. The beaded-edge wheels were replaced in June of that year by wellbase rims.

The engine/gearbox unit and rear axle being fitted in 1925 to a Cowley chassis on a labour-intensive assembly track that would not be mechanised until 1934. Unlike the pre-war cars which had a Rubery Owen frame, these were built up from pressings produced in Belgium.

Occasional Four and four-seater by a two-piece screen. A Cowley Van, in Standard and De Luxe forms, was introduced; its bodies were prefabricated by Davidson of Trafford Park, Manchester, and it was assembled at Cowley.

Morris's 1925 output of 47,138 Bullnoses represented an astonishing 36 per cent of British car production although he would never again enjoy such a commanding position within the motor industry. Profits of £1,556,000, recorded for a fifteen-month period, also broke the million-pound barrier for the first time.

The Cowleys were outwardly similar to the previous year's cars although changes had taken place beneath the surface. The chassis with its 1915 origins was strengthened and the long-running beaded-edge wheels were replaced by wellbase rims although front-wheel brakes were still not specified.

The body range was refined, with the four-seater tourer now fitted with a new simplified hood and single upright sticks. A Cowley-built two-door saloon, introduced in mid season, had a door on each side whilst the two-seater touring body was redesigned, being flush-sided at the rear to accommodate a larger dickey seat. A

Cowleys about to leave the factory on a road test in 1925. The slave bodies with their minimum of protection were purely temporary fitments and the absence of bonnets permitted unrestricted access to the engines.

23

The chassis and bodies united. Note on the left the De Luxe van body that was assembled at Cowley from parts made by Davidson of Trafford Park, Manchester.

Cars nearing completion in the erecting shop in 1925, with the Oxford line on the left and the Cowley one on the right. Note the absence of saloons, as these were then made by Morgan of Leighton Buzzard, Bedfordshire. The Cowley factory, however, took over in 1926.

A 1925 Cowley Occasional Four with Wicklow registration. The boxes on the nearside running board contained, from left to right, tools and battery respectively.

A 1926 Cowley tourer with front-wheel brakes but still with no offside doors. The 2 gallon (9.09 litre) petrol can on the running board was stamped on the top 'For Morris Cars Only. Non returnable'. Shell provided the can and its contents free to Morris in return for him recommending the fuel to Bullnose owners.

fixed-head coupé was introduced in mid season.

1926 was destined to be the Bullnose's last year, despite a record 48,503 being produced. Outwardly the open cars were similar to the previous season's although external door handles were fitted for the first and only season on the Cowley. The saloon now had its doors only on the nearside. Front-wheel brakes were at last standardised on the Cowley although rears only could still be specified on the open cars.

In August the Bullnose was replaced by the so called Flatnose models although the last of the older cars did not leave Cowley until December. In all 147,724 Bullnoses had been built since 1919. A total of 3568 vans and 568 chassis were also completed in 1924–6.

The Cowley and Oxford names were perpetuated on the Flatnose range, which later accommodated Pressed Steel saloon bodywork. Although more popular, some 185,000 being built, the Flatnose nevertheless lacked the ingenuity and flair that had made the Bullnose Morris the British motor industry's first bestseller.

This child's Bullnose Morris pedal car was LB Ltd's (Lines Brothers) No. 5 model, identifiable by its solid tyres. Sold by Gamages, it cost £4 17s 9d in 1927. There was a more expensive, No. 9 version, with balloon tyres, advertised as 'absolutely ripping', at £6.

25

A bedecked 1924 Oxford four-seater tourer in rural Cambridgeshire. Whatever was the occasion? The offside doors were peculiar to the Oxford and the three-piece windscreen was introduced that year. The car behind is a 10CV Citroen.

OXFORD REFINEMENT

The Morris Oxford was, in essence, a perpetuation of the well equipped and appointed Continental Cowley of 1915. A considerably more profitable car than the post-war Cowley, its predecessor had not been fitted with an electric starter but this became a universal requirement on practically all cars after the First World War.

Morris's response was to look again across the Atlantic for inspiration and he opted for the dynamotor. Produced by Lucas, this bulky combination of starter and dynamo, although quiet, was never able to fulfil both functions satisfactorily.

Outwardly, the most obvious difference between the Oxford and its cheaper stablemate was the fitment of a five-lamp lighting set. Selling at £590 in 1920, the factory-built four-seater tourer was £65 more than its Cowley equivalent. The two-seater was by Hollick & Pratt, whilst a coupé, a coupé limousine and a fixed-head four-light coupé were all produced by Raworth in 1921–2 but thereafter Cowley-made.

Early in 1923, to counter the increasing weight of the Oxford, it was offered with a larger-capacity 1.8 litre engine although the Cowley continued with the original unit. Initially available as a 13.9 hp option, it was designated the Type CE by Morris Engines and shared the four-port exhaust arrangement introduced on the CB of 1922.

Although the 102 mm stroke was retained, the bore was enlarged to 75 mm, resulting in an increase in capacity to 1802 cc. The new engine developed 32 bhp,

At a time when houses were not designed to accommodate automobiles and a garage was where you took your car to be repaired, early in 1925 Bullnose owners were offered the Morris Motor House by the company. There were initially two versions, both with a wooden frame and asbestos 'fire-resistant' panels. This one was for the Cowley and cost £15 15s, whilst the Oxford owner was offered a larger design, with two more panels either side, at £17. They were produced, some with metal frames, for succeeding models and remained available until 1930.

26

The larger-capacity radiator and door handles arrived in 1924 on the open Oxfords. The lady is William Morris's secretary, Hylda Church, who in that year married the company's publicity manager, Miles Thomas, who later became vice-chairman of the business.

compared with 26 bhp for the smaller version, but the cars' 50 mph (80 km/h) top speed remained about the same although torque was much improved. The original 11.9 hp radiator was retained.

The 1.8 litre engine was standardised for the 1924 season and a larger-capacity radiator introduced. This, in turn, meant a taller and wider scuttle and, to cater for the attendant increased fuel consumption, the capacity of the petrol tank located within was increased from 5 to 7 gallons (22.7 to 31.8 litres).

Two new body styles were offered, a saloon and a cabriolet, both of which were made at Hamworthy, Dorset, by Chalmer & Hoyer, the manufacturer of Hoyal bodies. The saloon possessed one large door on either side of the body. External door handles were extended to all models; they had previously featured only on the more expensive coupé and cabriolet.

Another change that further separated the Oxford from its Cowley origins occurred for the 1925 season, when its wheelbase was increased 6 inches (152 mm) to 9 feet (2743 mm). The four-seater tourer was now, like the two-seater, produced by what had

The prospective owner of a 1924 Oxford in the showrooms of The Morris Garages' head office in Queen Street, Oxford. Note copies of 'The Morris Owner', edited by Miles Thomas, on the desk. The Boyce Motometer water temperature indicator in the car's radiator cap was used in the 1924 and 1925 seasons.

A quartet of Oxford saloons leads a crocodile of over fifty Morrises being delivered early in 1926 by drivers employed by B. J. Henry to the London agents Stewart & Ardern. The leading car has a blue pennant on its radiator cap bearing the S & A corporate monogram.

Right: *The Oxford acquired front-wheel brakes in the 1925 model year. Balancing the front brakes was effected by turning the wing nut fitted to the end of the rod which adjusted each pair of shoes. The model used 12 inch (305 mm) drums, in contrast to the Cowley's 9 inch (228 mm) ones.*

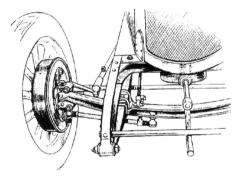

become Morris Bodies.

Initially the original 8 foot 6 inch (2590 mm) frame was retained for the two-seater and coupé although the new chassis was subsequently extended to all models. This permitted the introduction of an Oxford landaulette, also by Chalmer & Hoyer. Wellbase wheels, available as an option from 1924, replaced the beaded-edge variety.

In 1926, the last year of manufacture, two new models were introduced in the shape of a three-quarter coupé and a saloon landaulette. Otherwise the range closely resembled the previous year's cars.

No mention of the Morris Oxford would be complete without reference to the F-Type Oxford Silent Six, which entered production in 1922. It was, in effect, the side-valve 11.9 hp Bullnose unit with two extra cylinders. The internal dimensions were thus 69 by 102 mm, which gave 2320 cc. A 1921 prototype was fitted with a luxurious coupé body and run by Morris himself, the first of four examples he was to drive.

Mounted in an elongated chassis with a 9 foot 3 inch (2819 mm) wheelbase 9 inches (229 mm) longer than the Morris fours, the

Oxford chassis awaiting their coachwork in the erecting shop at Cowley. Powered by the Type CE 13.9 hp engine, these were painted blue to differentiate them from the 11.9 hp power units, which were finished in red.

A 1925 Oxford coupé outside the famous Lygon Arms hotel in Broadway, Worcestershire, as featured in a contemporary advertisement in 'The Morris Owner'. The vehicle behind is a Morgan three-wheeler.

A 1925 Oxford four-seater tourer at Brooklands with its owner, Miss Muriel Chiesman, cousin of Russel Chiesman, who was a friend of Cecil Kimber, general manager of The Morris Garages and creator of the MG marque. She had just won the Novice Cup for the best individual performance in an event staged by the Civil Service Motoring Association at the Surrey track.

17.9 hp Silent Six Oxford sold for £500 in four-seater touring form, £54 more than its four-cylinder equivalent. Wire wheels and half-elliptic rear springs were further departures from previous practice.

The factory intended to produce five hundred but the model unfortunately proved to be mechanically flawed as it soon became apparent that the engine suffered from periodic vibrations. These, in turn, resulted in the sparsely supported three-bearing

A 1925 Oxford tourer with the longer chassis shown to good effect and rear passengers protected by an Auster screen. The two-piece windscreen, now complete with wiper, replaced the previous year's three-piece one.

Although the Morris name disappeared in 1983, that of MG survives and until 1929 its models were directly based on Morris products. The two-tone body by Carbodies, triangulated windscreen mountings and scuttle-mounted ship's type ventilators distinguish this as a 1925/26 MG Super Sports. At £375, it cost a significant £90 more than the equivalent Oxford four-seater.

crankshaft succumbing to failure.

So demand for the Morris Six was minimal although the first open four-seater touring version was bought by Lord Redesdale, father of the celebrated Mitford sisters. Production, if that is the word, peaked in 1924 when just thirty cars left Cowley and it ceased in 1926. A total of fifty was completed.

But the failure of the F-type should not be allowed to cloud William Morris's phenomenal success. It was an extraordinary achievement for a self-taught mechanic and his cannily selected team. Regrettably, over the years he fell out with all the key players who had helped to make his business Britain's largest car company. This was one of many factors that led to the Morris name disappearing in 1983, just seventy years since the Bullnose had first taken to the road.

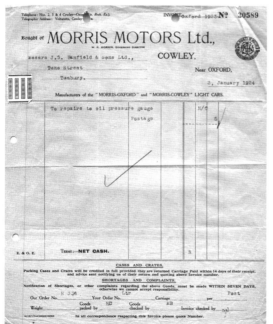

Morris Motors did not charge Banfield of Tenbury, Worcestershire, for repairs to an oil pressure gauge, probably because the car from which it came was still under guarantee, but did require payment of 5d for the postage incurred in returning the unit. It was such careful housekeeping that helped William Morris to become Britain's first motoring millionaire.

FURTHER READING

The acclaimed standard work on the Bullnose Morris by Jarman and Barraclough is unfortunately now out of print but copies, along with the older titles listed below, can often be found in specialist bookshops, at Autojumbles and club events catering for Morris vehicles.

Adeney, Martin. *Nuffield: A Biography*. Robert Hale, 1993.

Andrews, P.W.S., and Brunner, Elizabeth. *The Life of Lord Nuffield*. Basil Blackwell, 1955.

Edwards, Harry. *Morris Cars: The First 35 Years*. The Morris Register, 1978, 1984 and 1998.

Edwards, Harry. *The Morris Motor Car 1913–1983*. Moorland Publishing, 1983, and Roadmaster Publishing, 1997.

Garnons-Williams, Philip. *Morris Cars 1913–1930*. Published by the author, 1977.

Hull, Peter. *Lord Nuffield*. Shire, second edition 1993.

Jarman, Lytton P., and Barraclough, Robin. *The Bullnose Morris*. Macdonald, 1965.

Jarman, Lytton P., and Barraclough, Robin. *The Bullnose and Flatnose Morris*. David & Charles, 1977.

Jarman, L.P., and Barraclough, R.I. *The Bullnose Morris Cowley*. Profile Publications, no. 63, 1967.

Seymour, Peter J. *Morris Bullnose and Flatnose Power Units*. The Bullnose Morris Club, 1995.

Seymour, Peter J. *Morris Light Vans 1924–1934*. P and B Publishing, 1999.

The 1925 Cowley on the left belongs to the Bullnose Morris Club's publications officer, Donald Way. Note that its registration number is the digit prior to that issued to the Oxford saloon on the front cover of this book. Way's tourer is in company with a 1914 Oxford De Luxe.

PLACES TO VISIT

The following museums contain at least one Bullnose Morris but it is always advisable to check before making a journey.

Bristol Industrial Museum, Prince's Wharf, City Docks, Bristol BS1 4RN. Telephone: 0117 925 1470. Website: www.bristol-city.gov.uk

Haynes Motor Museum, Sparkford, Somerset BA22 7LH. Telephone: 01963 440804. Website: www.haynesmotormuseum.co.uk

Heritage Motor Centre, British Motor Industry Heritage Trust, Gaydon, Warwick CV35 0BJ. Telephone: 01926 641188. Website: www.heritage.org.uk

Lincolnshire Road Transport Museum, Whisby Road, North Hykeham, Lincoln LN6 3QT. Telephone: 01522 500566. Website: www.lvvs.freeserve.co.uk

Museum of British Road Transport, St Agnes Lane, Hales Street, Coventry CV1 1PN. Telephone: 024 76 832425. Website: www.mbrt.co.uk

National Motor Museum, Beaulieu, Brockenhurst, Hampshire SO42 7ZN. Telephone: 01590 612345. Website: www.beaulieu.co.uk

Shuttleworth Collection, Old Warden Park, Biggleswade, Bedfordshire SG18 9EP. Telephone: 01767 627288. Website: www.shuttleworth.org

Ulster Folk and Transport Museum, 153 Bangor Road, Cultra, Holywood, County Down, Northern Ireland BT18 0EU. Telephone: 028 90 428428. Website: www.nidex.com/uftm

Nuffield Place, Huntercombe, Henley-on-Thames, Oxfordshire RG9 5RY. Telephone: 01491 641224. This house, William Morris's Oxfordshire home for some thirty years, is open to the public on the second and fourth Sunday afternoons of each month between May and September.

The Bullnose Morris Club caters for Morris cars and commercials manufactured 1913–1930. Full details can be obtained from Chas Moody, 14 Holland Road, Oxted, Surrey RH8 9AU. Website: www.bullnose.org.uk

The Morris Register caters for Morrises of all ages, including the Bullnose, and information is available from Mike Thomas, 14 Meadow Rise, Horam, East Sussex TN21 0IZ. Website: www.morrisregister.co.uk

Members of the Bullnose Morris Club gathering at Nuffield Place, Oxfordshire, where Morris, who became Lord Nuffield in 1934, lived from that year until his death in 1963. The house is open to the public on some Sunday afternoons during the summer months.